PURE AT HEART 2

LEROY "STUFF" SMITH
(NAME)

326-12-5480   S-14029
S.S NO.   MBR. NO.

LeRoy "Stuff" Smith
(MEMBER'S SIGNATURE)

STUFF SMITH

PURE AT HEART 2

Anecdotes & Interviews

New Augmented Edition

Edited by
ANTHONY BARNETT

with further contributions by
MARY LEE HESTER
EVA LØGAGER
TIMME ROSENKRANTZ
ARLENE SMITH
VAL WILMER

A·B

Pure at Heart 2
The Human Side of Jazz
Copyright © Allardyce, Barnett 1991, 2002

Stuff Smith: The Genius of Jazz Violin & Photo
Copyright © Val Wilmer 1965, 2002
Stuff Smith: An Interview
Copyright © Anthony Barnett 1991, 2002
The Fellow with the Fiddle & About Uncle Henry
Copyright © Timme Rosenkrantz Archive 2002
I Hope Gabriel Likes My Music
Copyright © Arlene Smith 2002
A-damn in the God-damn of E-damn, 1966
Copyright © Eva Løgager 1991, 2002

In accordance with the Copyright, Design and Patents Act 1988
Hezekiah Le Roy Gordon Stuff Smith, Arlene Smith
Eva Løgager, Timme Rosenkrantz, Anthony Barnett, Val Wilmer
are hereby identified as the authors of their parts of this work
and Anthony Barnett as the editor of this work

All rights reserved. No part of this work may be reproduced
stored or transmitted by any means or in any form known
or as yet unknown except for brief quotations in reviews
without the written permission of relevant copyright holders
Address enquiries to the publisher

Published 2002 by
Allardyce Book imprint of Allardyce, Barnett, Publishers
14 Mount Street, Lewes, East Sussex BN7 1HL England
www.abar.net

Distributed in USA to the book trade by
SPD Inc
1341 Seventh Street, Berkeley CA 94710-1403
www.spdbooks.org

Distributed in USA to the music trade by
Cadence–NorthCountry
Cadence Building, Redwood NY 13679-3104
www.cadencebuilding.com

Typeset by AB©omposer in Centaur MT
Printed by ARowe in EUK

A CIP record for this book is available from
The British Library and The Library of Congress

ISBN 0 907954 34 0

Editor's Note
7

VAL WILMER
Stuff Smith: The Genius of Jazz Violin
9

ANTHONY BARNETT
Stuff Smith: An Interview
with the participation of Timme Rosenkrantz
17

TIMME ROSENKRANTZ
The Fellow with the Fiddle
(Stuff Smith at the Onyx Club)
37

STUFF SMITH
A-damn in the God-damn of E-damn
(Blues in the Night ~ That's the Glory of Love)
43

STUFF SMITH
About Uncle Henry
(Stuff Smith Slept Here)
47

STUFF SMITH & ARLENE SMITH
I Hope Gabriel Likes My Music
(God, Music and Mr Whiskey)
as told to Lynn Gordon nom de plume of Arlene Smith
53

STUFF SMITH
The Human Side of Jazz
(An Autobiographical Beginning)
61

Note about Smith's holograph
On viewed documents bearing Stuff Smith's formal signature such as
his 1964 Musicians Local 47 dues book signature shown on the half title
he signs Le Roy "Stuff" Smith, less often LeRoy, though never Leroy
and here we defer to his preference

Photos

Cover previously unpublished photo of Stuff Smith while recording with
Stéphane Grappelli, Paris, 4 May 1957, courtesy Herman Leonard

Frontispiece photo of Stuff Smith by
Anthony Barnett, evening of ?21 April 1965

Page 10 previously unpublished photo with verso
of Stuff Smith taken with Smith's Poloroid camera by Val Wilmer
Regent Palace Hotel, London, 26 April 1965, courtesy Val Wilmer

Page 18 previously unpublished photo of AB and Stuff Smith by
Roger Kendrick, Regent Palace Hotel, 28 April 1965

Page 16, 38, 60 photos of Stuff Smith & Timme Rosenkrantz by
Anthony Barnett, Annie's Room, rehearsal, afternoon of 21 April 1965

Page 44 photo of Stuff Smith & Eva Løgager
unidentified location, September 1967, courtesy Eva Løgager

Page 48 photo of Smith's father C. T. "Pappy" Smith with fellow
barber-musicians Bob Foster, Bob Matthews, Charlotte, NC, c.1890s
printed in Down Beat 21 October 1946, courtesy Stuff Smith
also reprinted in Desert Sands, 1995

Page 52 previously unpublished photo of Stuff Smith & Arlene Smith
Stockholm, August or September 1965, courtesy Arlene Smith

Page 54 previously unpublished photo of Stuff Smith & Mary Lee Hester
unidentified nightclub, circa 1960, courtesy Mary Lee Hester

Page 62 photo of Stuff Smith with Blue Streak & White House by
Eva Løgager, Camp du T.C.F., outskirts of Paris, June 1967

Page 71 previously unpublished photo of Stuff Smith from the last
photo of Smith taken with Løgager family members before leaving for
Munich, Horsens, soon after mid September 1967, courtesy Eva Løgager

The 1991 edition of this book also includes two photos of Smith with AB and
with Doug Dobell at Annie's Room not reprinted here as well as six that are

NOTE

THE first edition of this little book, which appeared in 1991 under the shared editorship of myself with Eva Løgager, Smith's companion during his last period, paved the way for the two-volume Stuff Smith bio-discography *Desert Sands/Up Jumped the Devil* (1995/1998). This new edition benefits from research for those volumes, allowing a few errors and uncertainties to be set straight. Three new pieces have been added—a previously unpublished transcription narrated by the Stuff himself; a periodical interview by Val Wilmer; and the first pages of a long-lost biography as told to, in fact written by, Lynn Gordon (nom de plume of Smith's fourth wife Arlene Carolynn Smith—Gordon being Smith's given middle name) rediscovered by Mary Lee Hester who had begun preparing the typescript from the manuscript.

Val Wilmer's interview, taken by hand at Smith's London hotel when he was appearing at Annie Ross's club Annie's Room, is especially important because Wilmer asked the right questions. For example, Smith describes the Stroh-type violin he used with Alphonso Trent when making electrical recordings for Gennett; and explains the why and wherefore of dividing up his strings to parallel the brass and reed sections of a large orchestra.

By contrast, my own interview, recorded two days later, does not always ask the right questions. Certainly, there are occasions when the opportunity to delve deeper was missed because salient points were not recognized. Thirty-five years on I have a better idea of the questions I would like to have asked. Nevertheless, as will be seen, it is not without its jewel-like moments.

Timme Rosenkrantz's *Down Beat* recollection of Smith at the Onyx Club is slightly revised in light of the discovery of the original typescripts in English and Danish. As an aside, it might be worth mentioning that his closing anecdote, attributed to Heifetz and Smith, has since appeared in Warren Vaché Sr's *Mississippi Rag* interview with violinist Al Duffy, "The Forthright Fiddler from Brooklyn", friendly with Smith in the 1930s–1940s, except there Duffy attributes the anecdote to Heifetz and Rubinoff. We may never know whether the whole thing is apocryphal or not but for my money I'll settle with Heifetz–Hez—it rings funnier if not necessarily truer.

When we first printed Smith's classic story about Adam and Eve, transcribed from a 1966 birthday tape for fortuitously named Eva Løgager, we thought it might have been entitled "That's the Story of Love". But that was a misreading of Smith's handwriting on a tape box. In fact, it reads "That's the *Glory* of Love". Because the tape in question was not in this box, we are still not sure whether this is a title for our story—or for some other erased recording—but we think it should be because it is a line from Mercer-Arlen's "Blues in the Night" with which Smith invariable closed proceedings. Since the original printing, a 1944 article in *View, The Modern Magazine* has come to light in which Barry Ulanov gives a firsthand account of Smith's narration of the story at the Onyx. We have taken a few pointers including the orthography of Smith's Adam in Eden but we stick with God- rather than Ulanov's Gard- because of how we think it sounds on the tape. We might be wrong.

Smith's autobiographical party piece "About Uncle Henry", lapsing into goonish psuedo-surrealist absurdity, is found on a 1944 lacquer disc recording labelled "Stuff Smith Slept Here". Previously unpublished it was, however, once broadcast on Danmarks Radio in a Rosenkrantz memorial to Smith under the former title. The whereabouts of another party disc entitled "Inez Slept Here", presumably recorded on the same occasion, is currently unknown. The apparent tragic circumstance surrounding the death of Timme Rosenkrantz's companion of many years Inez Cavanaugh is noted in *FB: VIS, iv, 11*.

Arlene Smith's Lynn Gordon typescript "I Hope Gabriel Likes My Music" dates, she feels, from 1957 at the earliest. It breaks off in mid-sentence—many manuscript pages appear irretrievably lost but Dan Herbert's Arlene Smith *Desert Sands* interview goes some way towards restitution—yet reveals more than a little of Smith's love of life—and alcohol. The subtitle is new for this first printing. Beware: do not imbibe immoderately. It's fun but fraught.

In 1967 Eva Løgager began recording Smith's autobiography, which he thought should be entitled "The Human Side of Jazz", with the intention that it would be transcribed and edited by AB. Unfortunately, in the event, only one short tape, in three sections, was made before he died. The introductory character of this fragment, in which typically he self-effacingly prefers to talk mostly about his colleagues, should be born in mind. Even so, Smith recounts some hilarious and fascinating episodes and makes pithy observations which show another, more serious, side.

I would like to renew my thanks to Eva Løgager for her kindness in helping to gather the contents of the first edition of this collection of material by and about Hez, as he was known to many of his friends. None of it is printed in *Desert Sands* and indeed there are other odds and ends we might have included here had space allowed—rueful, semi-autobiographical lyrics, bawdy song parodies (we can't really call them lyrics), and unpublished and fugitive autobiographical quotes—that must await another occasion.

For material gathered here for the first time I offer my sincere thanks to Arlene Smith and Mary Lee Hester for the recovered typescript; to Val Wilmer for kind permission to reprint her article; to Arnvid Meyer for access to the Timme Rosenkrantz Archive when it was housed at the Danish Jazz Center; and to Frank Büchmann-Møller at the Music Department of Odense University Library where the archive is now housed.

AB, Lewes, February 2002

STUFF SMITH

THE GENIUS OF JAZZ VIOLIN

An Interview in Profile by
VAL WILMER
with material taken by hand at
Regent Palace Hotel, London
26 April 1965

Published as
Stuff Smith: The Genius of Jazz Violin
Talks to Valerie Wilmer
in Jazz Beat
London, June 1965

Newly Edited by VW
Footnotes by AB

To Valerie a real fine lady, who really knows Jazz & the beat. also a great writer She really knows her changes — Your Swinging Friend
Stuff Smith
4/26/65,
Annie's Room London Eng.

THE last time he visited Britain Duke Ellington featured parts of his evocative suite, *Black, Brown and Beige*. And each time Ray Nance fondly brought his violin down front to add its eloquent voice to the "Come Sunday" theme, all the little girls in the audience started nudging their young men. These gentlemen, many comparative newcomers to jazz, shifted uneasily and loosened their collars. Violin jazz? What an anomaly!

Well, is it? Violins are in evidence in many of those faded photographs of stiff upper-lipped New Orleans orchestras, but nevertheless, the instrument has rarely been used in jazz since the inception of recording. Outstanding practitioners of the art of jazz violin can be counted on one hand—Joe Venuti, Eddie South, Ray Nance, Stéphane Grappelli, Svend Asmussen.

And then there's Stuff Smith. Stuff is the indisputable king of jazz violin, a swinger of the first degree who makes his fiddle sound like a horn. He uses the last six or eight inches of his bow to slur his notes in the manner of a wind instrument. "Using the end of the bow causes you to bow the way you breathe," he says. "It's my equivalent of a horn player's breath control."

For a fortnight recently, Stuff enchanted habituees of Annie's Room with his singing, playing and mugging. He has the kind of energy that belongs only to musicians who grew up in the early days of jazz when you had to work hard to entertain—or else. At 56 he acts like a man ten or fifteen years younger and attributes this longevity to a state of mind, "I always put my music first, but these youngsters coming up, I don't know where they put it. They have their own conception of jazz. I don't criticise them but I don't respect them like I do Duke and Basie or Stan Kenton. The damndest band in the world is Duke's, don't let anybody kid you. That old man is something else!"

Stuff explained why so few musicians choose violin as a jazz instrument. "Their teachers don't allow them to play jazz, you see. They teach you Mendelssohn and all those violin concertos. I had lessons for six months but I always wanted to play what *I* wanted to play, and jazz was IT. Concert violin was a different feeling and it was too stiff for me. I liked something loose, something original. I can't see me playing somebody else's troubles!" he laughed. "Let me play my own—I get a kick out of that 'cause all my troubles are good ones!"

The violinist was born in Portsmouth, Ohio, in 1909 and first became interested in jazz after hearing Louis Armstrong's record of "West End Blues". "I'll never forget it," he recalls. "I was shining shoes in my father's barber shop and after that I started saving up my little pennies so I could get me one of those wind-up victrolas. I bought the record and I had good ears so I could play anything I heard. I soon learned the "West End Blues" and then I went out to this fishing platform behind our house where my father was playing the blues for a friend. I asked could I kinda play a little chorus in there and my father said, 'you can't play this kinda stuff'. I said, 'I can try, can't I?' So I did." [1]

Stuff's first important professional job was with a big band led by Alphonso Trent, and as far back as 1928 he and the drummer were trying out the idea of amplifying the violin through a speaker. In 1928 the Trent band recorded for Gennett in Richmond, Indiana, and Stuff recalled the primitive methods by which his instrument was recorded.

"The violin had a kind of speaker on it. The bridge was set on top of an aluminum business that looked like a chicken bone! At the end of the bone was a little hole with a very fine screw that ran into a real thin aluminum disc. This disc was padded with

---

[1] Smith is mistaken in citing "West End Blues"—and elsewhere "Savoy Blues"—as his early exposure to Armstrong. It was not recorded until 1928—and "Savoy Blues" in 1927—by which time Smith, although still a teenager, had been working as a professional musician since 1926. Smith has doubtless confused admiration for these recordings with recollection of first hearing Armstrong on recordings by King Oliver in 1923; cf. pp.19, 61-62; and "Stuff Smith & Louis Armstrong", *Desert Sands*, p.348.

fabric and tightened, and then when you hit the bridge the vibrations would go through this little screw into the disc and this would throw the sound out. This was the only way you could record with a violin because at that time the microphone wouldn't pick it up." [1]

Stuff started using a proper amplifier in the late 1930s but before then he would cut his bridge between the A and the D strings to increase the instrument's volume. "The old fiddlers used to slit it down like that. Another thing they used to do was get rattlesnakes' tails and dry 'em out and put 'em in the violin. That made a kinda vibration." [2]

The violinist was given his first electric instrument by the manufacturing company in exchange for publicising the combination. "It sounded all right but it was just a little too metallic," he said. "So I started using a mute. I cocked my mute between the D and the G instead of between the E, A, and the D and the G—the full mute. I just used half of my mute to get the kind of tone I wanted. Before they gave me an amplifier, though, I had often thought of building something similar." [2]

Of Eddie South, generally considered second only to Stuff in his command of jazz violin, Smith said, "He was great but he had more of a gypsy style and so he didn't swing too much. I mean real swing, the hard-hitting swing, the kind that makes you pat your foot." He continued: "I like Ray Nance for what he does but he doesn't swing, neither. He plays pretty and so does Grappelli, but I really like Svend Asmussen the best. He kinda swings every now and then!"

Stuff is a sprightly, intelligent soul. It is obvious that he thought out a long time ago what he was going to do with his maverick instrument. "I always listened to a big band with

[1] Smith is describing a Stroh violin or a derivation of one.
[2] Smith's endorsement of National Dobro Corp. "Vio-Electric", developed in 1936, appeared in *Down Beat*, 15 November 1939. An oft-reproduced photo of Smith outside the Onyx with a National amplifier has previously been thought to date from 1937 because of a Charles Peterson band photo of that apparent date visible on a billboard; cf. *Up Jumped the Devil*, pp.32–33.

brass and reeds and strings—never the small bands. I'd see how Fletcher Henderson and Don Redman and all those guys would make their arrangements. Duke, too. They'd have the brass talk to the reeds, and so I divided my violin up like that. The E and the A were the brass and the D and the G the reeds. That's the way I figured it and it gives me the effect I want. It makes the violin sound bigger if you're playing double-stops at times."

In the late '30s and early '40s when 52nd Street was the place where it all happened in New York, Stuff and trumpeter Jonah Jones co-led a famous sextet at the Onyx Club. With Cozy Cole on drums the unit made many records, first for Vocalion, then for Decca and Brunswick, and Varsity. Some of these have since beome collectors' items. The violinist and trumpeter specialised in a fast-moving jazz and comedy, and contemporary photographs depict them wearing battered top-hats on their heads and dated "jive" expressions on their faces. Legends of the Onyx days abound in jazz history and Stuff was only too willing to supply an anecdote or two.

"We were very young in those days, you know, so we had a ball," he laughed. "We had an arrangement on 'Stomping at the Savoy' that would last half an hour and we used to play it all the time. The people just loved it. Cozy Cole had on a little straw hat with the brim taken off and he had a little light fixed in the hat. The light would flicker as he shook his head and I used to get the tempo from that. Every time we played 'Savoy' we'd start off real soft and as we gradually played the volume would continue to raise.

"So one Sunday this fellow came in. He was an Englishman and he said in that accent, 'Oh Stuff, would you maind playing "Stomping at the Savoy", that bloody piece you play for so long!' So we went off into it and every time we got to a certain volume this cat would jump up and say 'Wow!' and turn round and give us a 20 dollar bill! I said, 'Keep playin', boys!' and every time he jumped up I'd say, 'Wow!' right back at him. Must have got about two or three hundred dollars off that cat!"

Stuff's unorthodox technique made him a focal point for many classical violinists during the Onyx days. "They would come by and listen all the time. They just wondered how I could play so crazy. I fingered my fiddle crazy, I bowed crazy, I made funny kind of tones (but they would fit), and sometimes I played with no tone at all! Kreisler used to come in and he'd sit in with us, too, but he played piano. He could play jazz and Heifetz, too. He'd play real crazy stuff on violin."

Today, the genius of jazz violin lives a pretty quiet life in Los Angeles.[1] When he is not playing he can usually be found fishing or swimming. "No golf for me," he declares, "Too much walking!" But in spite of that he is no slouch when it comes to working. He still manages to amaze his audience as he saws away at his instrument, producing the most astonishing variety of sounds. He carries three bows with him because he'll get through one in a week, but his strings last a surprisingly long time considering the punishment they receive.

In many ways Stuff Smith is unique. In his choice of instrument, in his attitude to life. Cheerful, youthful, entertaining— "Musicians are kind people," he maintains. He swings by implying the notes rather than voicing them and knows all there is to know about swinging, the essence of his kind of jazz. The violin in his hands takes on a new sound and a new appearance. it has never looked a particularly hip instrument; Hezekiah Le Roy Gordon Smith made it so.

[1] As it turned out, Smith did not return to Los Angeles but remained in Europe.

End

STUFF SMITH

An Interview

Recorded by
ANTHONY BARNETT
with the participation of
TIMME ROSENKRANTZ
at
Regent Palace Hotel, London
28 April 1965

Asterix denotes laughter
Ellipsis generally denotes indecipherable
asides on the low volume audio tape

Newly Edited by AB

FIRST, *I'd like to ask why you decided to play the violin when so many other musicians weren't.*

Well, I figured that, well, I'll tell you, to tell the truth really all I wanted to do was to play the "West End Blues", just like I told you before. My father wanted me to be a classical violinist because he had sent my sister to Oberlin Conservatory and she was about ready to graduate, and he wanted her and I to tour all around and play the classics, you know. But I had other little feet than that, man, you know, I didn't dig none of that issue and when I heard Louis Armstrong play "West End Blues" I said, Now here man, you know, that's the tone I want to hear, the sound, and the feeling, which made me feel good, you know. So I practised for a couple of months or so and Dad didn't know anything about it. This "West End Blues".[1]

Did you think of playing any instrument other than the violin?

Yeah. I wanted to play piano, really. That's true. And drums, and, you see, I sawed the neck off his banjo and and started beating the drums, oh * you know, took the strings off it, and, like, the door of my room was off. So he said, Now you play this violin. So he stuck it under my chin. I think it was a three-quarter size. * It was too large for me.[2]

Did you hear, when you were young, apart from your father, any violinists who influenced you in jazz?

Yeah, yeah. I heard Joe Venuti. Joe Venuti and Eddie Lang. I heard Joe Venuti and Eddie Lang. They came through our city, and they played at a saloon. And Dad says, Come over here, I

[1] cf. note, p.12 [2] cf. photo incl. Smith's father, p.48

want you to hear this violinist, you know, and this guitar. So *
they was playing good jazz. I thought, you know, I don't know
exactly what they are doing but I felt it. You know, one of those
things. I think jazz is due to the feeling. Same as all music is
nothing but feeling. It's the heart, the soul, the mind, and that's
what, I guess, life is.

When you left Johnson C. Smith University you joined a traveling musical troupe. Do you remember its name?

Yeah. Aunt Jemima Revue. That was the name of the show.

And the other musicians with you?

Well, King Swayze, and a saxophone player named Ikelberger *
. . . He played pretty nice sax, you know, alto sax. And we had a
trombone player we called Trombonski . . .

Did you play for dances, for stage presentation?

Just stage. . . . No, no dancing.

Were there any blues singers with the troupe?

No. Sammy Lewis was a singer. He was kinda, kinda * well, he
was a singer, yeah.[1]

Then you joined Jelly Roll Morton, or were there other troupes before?

No, I joined Trent. Alphonso Trent after that. Swayze left the
show, and he went and joined Trent, and then, when he got to

[1] Sammie [Sammy] Lewes recorded with the musicians cited six months before Smith joined the troupe; cf. *Desert Sands*, p.56.

Trent, Trent was going to do a hotel and he wanted waltzes, so he figured that he needed a violin.

What year was this?

Oh, I don't know, man * I don't know, man . . . It was after the first world war * yeah . . . it was back there. I joined Trent in Lexington, Kentucky. Then we went to Dallas. We played the Adolphus Hotel for about a year and two weeks. We played the big hotel in San Antonio and a smaller hotel in Houston. As a matter of fact we covered Texas thoroughly. The band, then, we played for dances, then. So Trent says, Stuff, you, you get in front of the band, you know. Trent was the leader. He was the pianist. Well, he wanted me out front because I just couldn't sit down in a chair and play, you know. I had to stand up and play my violin. * And then I can look at all the chicks too, and so that was real great.

But you did play with Jelly Roll Morton?

Well, after we left. After Swayze and I left Trent. We left Trent in Davenport, Iowa, and then we went straight into New York and joined Jelly Roll. Jelly Roll sent for Swayze, and Swayze got me in with Jelly Roll Morton. And we were playing five cents a dance. A club called the, Arcadia, uh, Alhambra Ballroom, on 125th and 7th Avenue.[1] So we played. I played with Jelly Roll for two weeks. And the band was too loud. And then I didn't like the way he talked to Chick Webb. 'Cause I thought Chick Webb was a great drummer. Yeah. And Chick had a band at the Savoy. So I figured, man, I'm going back to Trent where I can be heard. We didn't have no amplifiers then, you know. You understand?

[1] Smith almost certainly means the Rose Danceland a taxi dance school on 125th Street where Morton played 1927–1928. Swayzee played there with Morton at least in November 1928 and recorded in December after the engagement ended.

And they play a waltz. And these cats would play a waltz and play ⅝ time instead of ¾. You know, they kind of jazz it up. And you couldn't hear the violin. So I said, they don't need me. So I cut out and went back to Little Rock and joined Trent. And from there I stayed with Trent for about six more months and went to Buffalo.

You made some records with Trent.

Oh, yes, sure. Yeah. We made those in Richmond, Indiana.

Can we check the personnel? Does this check with what you remember? In 1928 the band's trumpets were Chester Clark, Irving Randolph.

No. In '28? Yeah. But before that. Now in '27. Now let me give you the personnel of the band: on trumpets was Chester Clark, King Swayze, and, that was the trumpets. And one trombone, Leo Mosley. * Now, on saxophones we had James Jeter, Lee Hilliard, and Hayes Pillars, no, Hayes, yeah, Hayes Pillars. Now that was the reed section. Now, and in the rhythm section we had Brent Sparks on tuba. Wait a minute, Brent Sparks on tuba and A. G. Godley on drums. And, yeah, Crook, on banjo. And Alphonso Trent on piano. And I played the violin.

On the first records Robert Eppie Jackson was tuba?

Eppie, Eppie. From Kansas City.

And when did Irving Randolph join the trumpet section?

Later. 'Cause Swayze went with Cab Calloway, yeah.

And then Peanuts Holland joined the trumpets?

Peanuts Holland. I got Peanuts the job in the band.

George Hudson?

George Hudson followed Peanuts. When we went back to St Louis and played on, no, we didn't, we played a dance in St Louis and we picked up George Hudson. And George, at that time, he didn't have a band.

Eddie Sherman came in on tenor?

That's when I cut out. See, I cut out then. I went back to Buffalo. I remember that 'cause my wife had a baby. * Had to go back to care for my son.

Do you remember the musicians in your Buffalo bands?

Yeah. On trombone . . . I had two of them. What do you mean, my eight piece band?

You had Joe Thomas on tenor at one time?

Yeah, well, that was a seven piece band. In my seven piece band at Ann Montgomery's Little Harlem. That was in Buffalo. She told me to bring in a band, and I did, you know. I went out and got some musicians. I had on trumpet, first trumpet player I had was Peanuts, * Peanuts Holland, on trumpet. Joe Thomas on tenor. Al Williams, no, Al Williams came in later after Joe went with Jimmie [Lunceford]. Let me see now. On trumpet I had Peanuts Holland. Well, I remember James Sherman on piano . . .

You made two more records with Trent in 1933. . . . With Gus Wilson on trombone?

But I wasn't with Trent then . . . Well, Gus Wilson was in my band.

The titles were "Clementine" and "I've Found a New Baby". With the violinist Anderson Lacey.

Ah, I wasn't with Trent then. No, no. See, Gus Wilson, I got Gus Wilson, that's Teddy Wilson's brother . . . Gus Wilson, good arranger, and everywhere he goes he makes an arrangement on "Clementine".

So you're not playing on those two records?

No, no.

After you left Trent and before you made "I'se a Muggin'" in 1936 did you make any other records?

No, no. My first record was in '36. That was for Vocalion.[1]

Do you recall the period leading up to your Onyx Club engagement?

Yeah. I played at Ann Mongomery's. And then I had a seven piece band there. And then I went into the Vendome Hotel, and then I had a twelve piece band. That's where, that's when I got hold of Gus Wilson on the trombone. Hm, I've forgottem all the guys' names. I had Jonah [Jones]. I had Jonah in the band.

---

[1] In a later conversation Smith recalled his participation in unreleased recordings by Zach Whyte, for Gennett in 1931.

In Buffalo?

Yeah. And Jimmie Lunceford told us to come into the Lafayette Theatre [New York]. And Harold Oxley was supposed to book us, you know, around the world. Now, what we call around the world is New York, Philadelphia, Baltimore, and Washington. That's around the world. In the music game. *

I've seen photgraphs of you and Jonah at the Onyx Club with a caption which says, Jonah's truckin' dance should never have gone beyond his version. What was special about the way he used to do it?

Ah, he had flat feet * . . .

[Small talk about the personnel of the Onyx Club Boys.]

You wrote "Crescendo in Drums".

I wrote that for Cozy [Cole] when Cozy went with Cab [Calloway]. * The dirty dog. I'll never forget that one. That's when we were in the La Salle Hotel [Chicago].

You didn't record again until . . .

. . . until I got the trio.

You recorded with Red Norvo.

Oh well, I played with Red Norvo. Yeah, yeah . . . Then I made a couple of records with a girl named Mary . . . played guitar . . . yeah, Mary Osborne . . . I'd sure like to hear them . . .

This was when you formed the trio with Jimmy Jones and John Levy?

Yeah.

What led you to form a trio without drums?

Well, I don't know. Everybody was using a trio, you know, and the loot was getting awful low * back in those days. You know what I mean, don't you. And the loot was getting awful low. So I was in Chicago and my old lady had just divorced me, and I had myself a new queen. I had a queen but, you know, I couldn't expose her, * you understand . . . People would be calling me Don Juan, that's why . . .[1] But I thought it would be best that I get strings. You know, piano is a string, and bass is a string. And, we never even had a rehearsal. John Levy who was a special delivery, a letter carrier in Chicago. And Jimmy Jones played ukulele. I didn't even know he played piano, you know. But he played beautiful chords on the ukulele. So I saw John Levy once there. I went to the Union. And the President says, I asked him, I says, I want to join it, and I want to get a trio. Now give me some good men, you know. So he says, Well, we got a good bass player here. He hasn't played for quite a while. He plays piano and bass. And then we have a pianist who's just come out of college. His name is Jimmy Jones. And I said, Well, you tell those guys to meet me at Eddie's Three Deuces. Now, I'm not talking about the old Three Deuces that we had in Chicago. This is the Three Deuces on Wabash. . . . So they met me there and I told them, I said, Meet me tomorrow night at nine, at quarter to nine. You must wear a black, blue or black suit, with a red tie and a white apron, and black shoes, and, you can go on about the rest . . . I looked at them and they looked at me and I said, Well, let's play "Crazy

[1] Dorothy Farrell, twice married to James T. Farrell, author of *Studs Lonigan*; cf. *Desert Sands*, pp.51–52,41; *Up Jumped the Devil*, p.27.

Rhythm", and Jimmy said, What key? I said, B flat. I said, Take four bars. And that was it. We seemed to gel right there.

[A confusing exchange about the personnel and chronology of some recordings in Chicago and New York printed in the first edition is omitted here.]

The V-discs in 1944.

Hm, that was back in New York . . . I made them when Charlie Barnet was up there. We made them there. I was in the army.

That was after the Asch session.

Yeah. sure.

Did you make other recordings for AFRS or for AFN?

Yeah, I think so, but, I don't remember. But I know I did. Because we were on the, not really the USO, we were Southern Bonds, you know. We sold lots of bonds in Chicago. War Bonds. I don't remember.

You composed "Stop—Look" on the way to the studio?

Yeah, walking down the street.

Someone nearly knocked you over?

Yeah.

And you made some records for Savoy which were never issued [at the time]?

Yeah, with Billy Daniels. Then I made one for Musicraft with Sarah Vaughan.

Any more at that time with Billy Daniels?

I think we did "Intermezzo", yeah.[1]

[Confusing small talk about the Town Hall and Times Hall concerts.]

Can you remember any other records you made during the 1940s?

Well, I can recall recording, in Chicago, with the trio again, but I don't know what company and I don't know what I played. I remember we had a couple of sessions there. On top of some great big old building out there. I've forgotten.[1]

You broadcast regularly during this period?

Oh yeah. Every night. We were on the air seven o'clock, seven, coast to coast.

Your own shows and other people's shows?

Yeah, yeah, but mostly our shows. We started, we stayed there a year then. We did pretty fair . . .

You've expressed great admiration for Duke Ellington and you've often recorded his compositions.

Yes, yes. Well, his compositions: there's a lot of something that

---

[1] There is no "Intermezzo" on the safety acetate of the complete session, but there is an apparently unallocated matrix.
[2] The World transcriptions and doubtless the session with Mary Osborne.

will live probably for ever, you know. Like the big composers. I put him in that class. Jazz speaking, and otherwise, Duke writes * practically anything you want to write. According to how Duke feels, I imagine. We'd never really sit down and talk but we've been pretty good friends for years . . . Yes, I have played with Duke.

Have you played duets with Ray Nance and the Duke Ellington Orchestra?

Yeah, I played, well, I played. * Ray and I, we always jive around. But we played Monterey Festival together and we played in New York.

Timme Rosenkrantz issued a recording with you and Lucky Thompson and Erroll Garner entitled "Test Pilots" which he recorded in his apartment.

. . . And I made a record with this girl that sings . . . Annie [Ross] sings just like her. I mean she's got the same style, this girl. She come out with the Five Spirits of Rhythm . . . A white girl. She sang beautiful, man. And she swung like mad. She never got the breaks she should have had. A pretty short girl.[1]

In the late 1940s Brunswick issued a recording: a version of "Desert Sands" coupled with "I Don't Stand a Ghost of a Chance". But this wasn't recorded as late as then?

No, we recorded it way before that.

With Jimmy Jones. Do you remember which session this was?

No. No, I don't.[2] How do you get all this information? *

[1] Ella Logan, Annie Ross's aunt. [2] From the 1943 World transcriptions.

There are books with some of the information. But much of it is inaccurate.

But that's true.

[Small talk about an erroneous journal reference to Smith's presence on 1947 recordings by Earl Hines; the violinist is Eddie South.]

In 1951 you recorded with Dizzy Gillespie. What were the circumstances?

Well, Dizzy came after me. * I knew Dizzy, you know. I knew Dizzy in New York.

What was your reaction to the young modern musicians—Dizzy Gillespie, Charlie Parker—during the mid 1940s?

Well, at that time, I thought they was very, very foolish. Because they were playing, playing notes that didn't fit in the cycle of, of chords. * You know. They was just playing all around the chords, in the chords, out the chords.

But your own music, your own music, was revolutionary. You played unusual things.

Yes, but, it was always, I'd fall back in that chord somewhere. *

You see, these cats would get out of that chord and stay out there, you know. And they called in bebop * . . .

And later you came to like it?

No. I never did like it.[1]

---

[1] Despite these protestations Smith and Gillespie were close; Gillespie credited Smith as a formative influence on him; cf. AB's essay acc. *The Complete Verve Stuff Smith Sessions* (Stamford, Mosaic Records, 1999), incl. 1957 recordings with Gillespie.

But you recorded with Dizzy.

Yeah, but Dizzy didn't play no bop then. Not when I recorded with him. 'Cause I made the arrangement on "Caravan" that he, that I made with him. And they played very fine. He had the bass player with the Modern Jazz Quartet . . .

Percy Heath.

Yeah. And then he had this other guy who plays vibraphone . . .

Milt Jackson.

Yeah, Milt Jackson was playing piano.

And he played organ on one track, "Time on My Hands"? [1]

Oh, probably so. I didn't play on that, did I?

Yes.

Yeah? Maybe I did. See, there you go, you see.

There are very few recordings by you during the early 1950s. There's the New York Phythian Temple concert in 1953. Nothing else until you recorded with Ella Fitzgerald in 1956. What were you doing during those years?

Playing around. Fishing. Having a ball. *

You were on the West Coast by 1956?

---

[1] Probably the Lowrey Organo, a five-octave keyless electronic organ piano-attachment operated via the piano keyboard as piano is also heard, and Lewis sings, on this title. Claude Jones recorded on organo with Eddie South the same year.

Yeah, I got married. That's what messed things up. I, I, wait a minute, Arlene, I didn't mean that, baby. * I mean, oh dear, I got married. * [1]

Did you enjoy recording with Ella Fitzgerald?

Oh, very much, very much. She's as sweet as she can be. And Ben [Webster], and Ben played something fine. And Paul Smith and, who was the drummer?

Alvin Stoller.

Yeah, right. He plays real great, man. He's got a beautiful beat. He don't lose no tempo, hm. And the bass player was great. I've forgotten the bass player's name, but he's a good man.

Joe Mondragon.

Yeah, that's him. An Italian fellow . . .

About a week later you recorded with Nat Cole.

Ah, there was a session! There's a boy, man. He can play all the piano you want to hear . . .

And Lester's brother Lee Young was on drums.

Yeah, he played beautiful. I mean to me, you know. Some guys just kind of fit you, you know, and other guys just don't fit you. But he fitted me, and I, what the hell, they don't have to fit me, let me fit them, man! The way they was playing, you know, go,

[1] Arlene Smith joined Stuff Smith in Paris in the summer but they separated in Copenhagen shortly afterwards.

man, shoot. Nat King Cole was one of the finest piano players in the country. I mean, for swinging, man. And, you know, he had so much in his heart, man. Nat really didn't want to sing. * He wanted to have a group. Nat wanted to play piano, I think! I might be wrong. Commercially speaking, it was a good thing he sang. You know, to make some loot. Well, loot's great. All I want is enough loot to just be comfortable. You know. Get what I want. You know. I don't want too much. You know. I just want to get me, what I want. You know. Maybe a couple of suits or something. To look decent when I walk out. And if I want to buy my friends a little, a dinner, or something like that, I ain't going to say, No ... which would spoil my appetite. But that's all. That's the way King Cole was, you know. I think he was that way. And, by the way, John Levy used to handle King Cole before he even got out of high school. * So John Levy was a hell of a manager, and he still is. If I could think of this girl who sings in America now that's real tops. She's the top singer now. John Levy's got her. What's her name?

Nancy Wilson?

Nancy Wilson. That's who I'm talking about. That's the top singer in America.

~ *Enter Timme Rosenkrantz* ~

TR = *Timme Rosenkrantz; Stuff Smith* = ST

When did you first visit New York?

TR: 1934.

And when did you first meet Stuff?

TR: I guess it must have been . . . 1936. he was at the Onyx at the time.

You spent a lot of time around 52nd Street?

TR: Well, in those days I spent more time uptown because I was living there. And there's where everything happened. The Onyx was the only place downtown really where they had good music, you know, except for the Dixieland bands, you know, which were all right if you liked that kind of music, which I did when I could have my beer with it. Dixieland and beer go very well together.

ST: But the best joint to go to after the Onyx closed was Timme's house . . .

TR: You say, Joint? . . . My apartment . . . My home! Not a joint!

ST: All the musicians used to say, Let's go to Timme's. That's all we had to say. And then about twenty of us would go to Timme's. And we used to drink Pernod and drink, er, other things. And eat. And Inez [Cavanaugh] would fix us some spaghetti and hamburgers. And Timme would be back there recording. You understand me? *

TR: Yeah . . . *

ST: What's that girl's name that I made those records with and you lost?

TR: Ella Logan.

ST: Ah, there! Ella . . . Yeah, that was a singing little girl . . .

TR: . . . She was real, variety, you know, artist. A real artist, you know . . . Entertainer . . . She never did much recording. I don't know why because she was, she was tops . . .

ST: That's what I'm trying to tell him now. Ella Logan was something else.

Ella Fitzgerald sang with you at the Onyx?

ST: No, I had Billie Holiday . . . Ella used to work for me on that program. You remember, Timme . . . They had Edgar Sampson, part of Cab's band, part of Chick's band, and my rhythm section. With Jonah.

TR: Well, I wasn't there at the time, I think.

ST: . . . [?]Thompson . . . [?]Thompson . . . was the Union big boss.
TR: I kept going back to Denmark . . . Then I came back in '39 and stayed all during the war years.

ST: We had, we had that whole program for about seven weeks. And I had about a fourteen piece band.[1]

TR: One of the best things I ever heard Stuff play was on the *Mildred Bailey Show.* You know, Stuff was a good friend, of course, of Mildred . . . It's on there. It's on that tape . . . The tape I've just, you've got on your lap.

[1] Airchecks of some of Smith's 1937 *Let's Listen to Lucidin* broadcasts are extant; cf. p.63; and *Up Jumped the Devil*, pp.48–50.

ST: Oh man. You want to hear some violin you must cut this thing off. Now, don't you think that's enough interview?

As you like.

ST: All right. Now, can I say, can I say the ending? May I put the ending on the interview? Tony Barnett,[1] you have really been a very, very fine friend of mine in London. Timme and I probably couldn't get along without you. You understand. But I still want to see the Queen's Jewels.

I'll take you to see the Queen's Jewels.

ST: That's good.

TR: But, you know, you, you can't take them out with you. You understand that?

ST: I didn't, I, I didn't say the *Jewels*.

TR: Oh.

ST: Yeah. *

TR: I'll see you later.

[1] Caution! Only Stuff Smith was allowed to call your editor Tony, cf. *Up Jumped the Devil*, p.26.

End

THE FELLOW WITH THE FIDDLE

STUFF SMITH AT THE ONYX CLUB

Published as
Reflections: Stuff Smith at the Onyx Club
by
TIMME ROSENKRANTZ
Down Beat, Chicago
3 January 1963

Edited by AB
from the published version
and the original typescripts
The Fellow with the Fiddle
translated by the author
from his original Danish
Stuff med Violinen
in the Rosenkrantz Archive
Odense Universitetsbibliotek

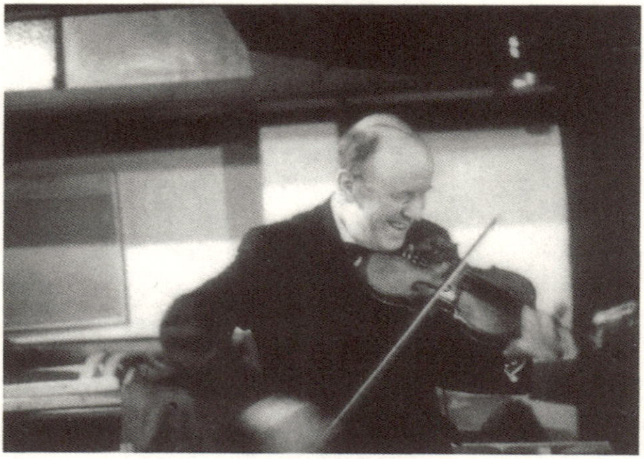

I*n* the late 1930s the Onyx Club was the place to go in New York. The clientele was made up mostly of musicians. The host and owner, Joe Helbock, was a former musician and always showed good taste in hiring bands.

It was here at the Onyx on my first visit to America that I heard the wonderful Spirits of Rhythm. It was here the John Kirby band was born and where Maxine Sullivan made her début. And one of the greatest things that happened at the club was the wonderful music of fiddler Stuff Smith and his band that featured Jonah Jones.

It was at the Onyx that I first met Hezekiah Le Roy Gordon Smith, known as Stuff, and that was something to be thankful for because Stuff Smith is surely the one musician who made the greatest impression on me—a great creative musician who should be placed, I feel, among the top jazz improvisers like Louis Armstrong, Fats Waller, Coleman Hawkins, Art Tatum and Lester Young. It is significant that all the jazz greats have the highest respect for Stuff, whereas laymen and most jazz fans hardly know him at all. Let's hope that the A&R men, when they get their hearing-aids adjusted, will rediscover him and record him.

Being a frustrated but violent violin player myself, I have heard most of the jazz fiddlers from Joe Venuti on. Even in little Denmark we have a guy who's a helluva man on fiddle, Svend Asmussen. But Stuff tops them all. When he takes over he just carries you away at once.

One should hear him *in natura*, this little, nimble, agile fellow, who jumps and dances and almost stands on his head when he plays and saws on his fiddle. He is irresistible—and it is probably only because of his lack of restraint, and his more or less bohemian nature, that he isn't better known today as a great jazz sensation or a television star. But with him, you never know what's going to happen. He is probably the cause of several gray hairs on the heads of many American club owners. I'll never forget him at the Onyx. All of a sudden, while his band was playing, he would disappear and you might find him in either the men's or the ladies' room playing a pretty solo to the local authority, or he might go to the bar and quench his thirst with a great inhalation of firewater. Often at the Onyx, after the music started, he would begin to tell *risqué* stories over the microphone. There was one about Adam and Eve in the Garden of Eden that used to make the management panic.

I've seen him stop in the middle of a solo when a young and beautiful lady entered the room and point out to the audience the lady's fine and fashionable anatomical qualities, which remarks sometimes registered unfavorably with her escort. But that didn't stop Stuff. He kept on and then he would play a dazzling chorus on his violin as if to emphasize what he had just said.

During the war years Stuff had founded a little trio—well, it wasn't smaller than any other trio—in fact, one might say it was bigger, because it consisted of Stuff and two wonderful musicians, Jimmy Jones on piano and John Levy on bass.

To my mind, this was one of the finest ensembles jazz has ever given us, and it was a great hit at the new Onyx where people came from outer space to listen to it. By then, the club had moved across the street after Joe Helbock had sold it. It was Swing Street and the whole joint was jumpin'.

Red Norvo and his wife at the time, the wonderful Mildred Bailey, were quite mad about Stuff and his music. Red had a band across the street at the Down Beat Club but each intermission, and very often too when he didn't have an intermission, he went over to listen to Stuff.

At that time, Mildred had a weekly show on CBS. It was

more or less a jazz show, and she presented all the jazz greats. Paul Baron's large orchestra with, among others, Charlie Shavers, Teddy Wilson and Specs Powell, and, of course, her own inimitable voice. It was quite a show!

Many times she had asked Stuff to play on the show. But he was quite shy about it and said he didn't like too many people—she had more than thirty in the band alone, including strings.

But she managed to convince him.

It was arranged that he should come two hours before the show went on the air so they would have ample time to rehearse.

There was no Stuff for the rehearsal and Mildred almost went out of her mind. But she kept Baron and everyone waiting to the last minute, and at 8.30 sharp—the time the show was to start—there was Hezekiah Stuff Smith in front of the band, as if he had been shot up through the floor. He played "Bugle Call Rag" as it never had been played before and never has since. He fell in at all the right places, and the orchestra, audience, and Mildred fell out. I know, because I was there! [1]

Stuff is what one might call a natural musician. He's never taken a formal lesson since he was a little child. He just figured it all out by himself, and though he may not play the fiddle the way it was meant to be played, what he does with it is quite fantastic.

I often saw old, long-haired symphony men, first violinists from the big radio symphony orchestras, sit at the Onyx and listen carefully to his playing. They were thrilled and fascinated by what they heard, and they asked themselves and everybody else, "How is it possible? How does he do it?"

Many of them were ready to swap their whole classical training for just a little bit of what Stuff possessed.

[1] Smith was present for the dress rehearsal. Both dress rehearsal and broadcast performances of this title are extant.

I had an apartment not very far from Swing Street at that time—7 West 46th Street, to be exact. Quite often, after the clubs on 52nd Street closed, the boys would come to my place with their instruments and wives and what have you, and there would be jamming until the wee hours of the morning. A lot of wonderful music was played, especially by Stuff, who came practically every night.

I had two very comfortable easy chairs. One was for Stuff to relax in after our sessions ... and he would be sitting there when I woke up in the afternoon. The other one was for Erroll Garner, but we'll go into that later.

The house at one time had belonged to Diamond Jim Brady, but when I lived there, it belonged to Stuff Smith.

Stuff's winning personality and sense of humor had endeared him to practically everyone he met. At this time he was well known at New York radio studios—he had become quite popular at the stations. For instance, here's a wonderful story I was told:

Jascha Heifetz was to play a concert at NBC. He took the main elevator, but the elevator man stopped him when he saw the violin case, and said, "Sorry, Mister! If you are going up to play, you'll have to take the personnel elevator in the back. This one is reserved for the public."

Heifez of course was highly insulted and angrily replied, "My good man, I am sure you don't know who I am. I am Jascha Heifetz!"

To this the elevator man answered, "Sorry, sir. Even if you were Stuff Smith, you'd still have to take the personnel elevator."

End

A-DAMN IN THE GOD-DAMN OF E-DAMN

BLUES IN THE NIGHT

THAT'S THE GLORY OF LOVE

Narrated & recorded by
STUFF SMITH
on or before Eva Løgager's birthday
Århus, Denmark
15 June 1966

"And what did you do, A-damn in the Gar-damn of E-damn?" And thus does Stuff Smith apostrophize the story of creation, nightly, except Tuesdays, at The Onyx, the neatest, cleanest, best-behaved of 52nd Street's homes of hot jazz. Stuff makes this inquiry in the course of an elaborate paraphrase of the lyrics of "Blues in the Night", which begins with the train whistle, "A-hooey de-hooey", which Stuff reads, "A fooey on who-ey?" and answers, "A fooey on Dewey [Thomas E.]" or on anybody named "Looey." It begins with the fooeys, lapses crazily into the story of A-damn and Ma-damn A-damn, and ends as the aboriginal couple bite into the apple. "Yum, yum; yum yum," Stuff sings, "Yum yum; yum, yum," four to the measure. "Yum, yum; yum, yum," and he picks up his fiddle. And he's off.
– Barry Ulanov, "Jazz of this Quarter",
View, The Modern Magazine
New York, December 1944

Transcribed by AB

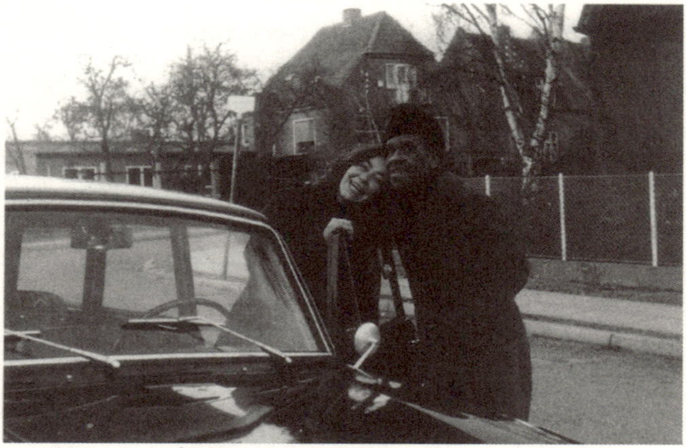

When A-damn was in the God-damn of E-damn he was havin' a ball. He had everything he wanted. He had chickens, gooses, couple of geeses, horses, cows. Till the bull come along. That was competition for the cows. But he had everything he wanted. He even had a little stream that ran through the God-damn of E-damn. And the sun used to shine down on this stream, you know, this little brook, the sun, brook, the brook, the sun, sun, brook, Sunny Brook! Huh. That's a drink they have these days called Sunny Brook. He even had some of that. And every morning he would go down there and get himself a little dipper of Sunny Brook until he drank so much of this Sunny Brook until he got the ulcers. So he decide I better get a new kick. So he looked upon a mountain with his binoculars that he had invented and there he saw Mount Mary's-y'-Mama. So he ran up to Mount-Mary's-y'-Mama and there was some green grass growing with little brown seeds on it. So he plucked all the seeds off and smashed them all up. Put them in a piece of brown paper he had invented and made him a roach about two yards long. Huh, huh. Well, instead of that cat walking over the God-damn of E-damn he started floating over the God-damn of E-damn. So he floated on back there by the brook and lay down and went to sleep. Finally, he woke up. And there she was. Ma-damn A-damn. Miss Eve. She stood over that boy's head and said, "Get up, you square! I'm going to put your boots on and lace them way up to your gills." Now A-damn had never seen nothin' like that before. So he jumped up. He said, "Hell-o babes!" She said, "Now lookey here. You go out to the orchard by that apple tree and when you get there you pluck one o' them big apples and bring it back to me." A-damn looked at her straight in the eyes and said, "Ney, ney. Forbidden fruit. Forbidden fruit." Ma-damn A-damn said, "Hey, hey. Juicy fruit. Juicy fruit." So A-damn, like a square, went on out there where the apple was parked on this tree. When he got there he saw a great big reptile. A snake. A' asp. Well, this as-s-k has his asp wrapped all around this tree. So he looked at him in the eyes. he said, "A-damn. Pluck one of these apples. Run up on Mount-Mary's-y'-Mama. Get yourself some o' that jive. Run back to old Eve and gas that chick." And that's exactly what he did. Took the apple. Great big red fat juicy apple. Went on up Mount Mary's-y'-Mama. Ran back to Eva and said, "Pick up, Jack." She looked at him. Took the apple. Put it in her hand and said, "A-damn, are you going to bite this apple this morning?" A-damn didn't say a word. She looked at him again and said, "A-damn, are you going to bite this apple this morning?" A-damn didn't say a word. She said, "Look here, A-damn." She said, "Are you going to stick one tooth in this fine foxy fruit this morning?" Well . . . Did he bite it? Yum, yum; yum yum. Did he bite it? Yum, yum; yum, yum. And that's why they leave you, leave you. Leave you with the Blues in the Night. 'Tain't right. 'Tain't right. 'Tain't right. . . . There you are, Eve!

End

ABOUT UNCLE HENRY

STUFF SMITH SLEPT HERE

A party piece narrated by
STUFF SMITH
Recorded by Timme Rosenkrantz
at his apartment
7 West 46th Street New York
between August–December 1944

First printed in
Shuffle Boil, A Magazine of Poets & Music
no. 2, Berkeley CA, summer 2002
Listening Chamber

Italic denotes interjections by
Timme Rosenkrantz, Inez Cavanaugh
& others unidentified
Ellipsis denotes hilarity
& incidental or indecipherable asides

Transcribed by AB

...This cat was standing out behind your house playing the guitar?...

No! You got it all wrong.... This is the truth. This is absolutely the truth. Really and truly I'm not kiddin'. This is the truth. *First, how old were you Stuff? Four years old?* Here I am, four years old. You understand me? *Tonight or then?* Right. Then. I was four years old. Then. And I was livin' in Massland ... Massillon, Ohio. That's, let me see, eight miles from Canton, thirty-two miles from Akron, fifty-four miles from Cleveland. That's where I was livin'. So you see I was three stops in front of Cleveland. You understand? Yeah. *Now we know.* That's where I was. Believe me? And, I, my daddy, my daddy, my father, when I say my daddy I mean my father, you understand?... That's what I'm tryin' to tell you, see. My father had himself a great little barbershop on the corner of 322 West Main Street, in Mass'lon. But behind the house was a garage. There was Uncle Henry. That's where Uncle Henry was. What am I talkin' about! *He's the guy who played the guitar, isn't he?* That's the man who played the guitar. But my father played the flute, at that time. As a matter of fact, he could play the flute *and* the guitar.... Put the light on, so I know what I'm doing there. I got to see the script.... So guess what happened! *E-e-vry* night, every single night, every single night, we would go down to Uncle Henry's for a plateau.... Uncle Henry was the man who did all the fishin' with his plateau. *What fishing? You didn't say anything about fishing?* I'm trying to tell you. There was a river runnin' there called the Tuskarawas River. Indian river. It was the Indian river. I know. I know, 'cause I was there. You understand me? Yeah. And he built his little plateau outside of the river.... And we used to go fishin'. *What did the fish say?... I didn't want a plateau...* I, the fish didn't say that at all. The fish didn't say that at all. You know what happened after that? All his jive was on this ... Mama would be home asleep and dad would step out for his little dandelion wine. And I was about behind him. What did I say? Behind him? Yeah. And he would start playin' his flute. You understand me? He would play this flute and Mr Henry, Uncle Henry, rather, rath-*or*, he would play the guitar and the mandolin. So there I am out there with the violin and don't know nothin' and I'm just lookin' for these fish. So all of a sudden we'd be playin' like mad and we'd get a strike—I thought I was baboosed there for a while. . . . So, but the man pitched me two balls . . . No, really. The man pitched me two balls and I said that's great. . . . But when he throwed me three balls I said, that is very different from all the rest. So he said, I'm pitchin' you four balls. Take a walk. I said, I think I need it, don't you? But he didn't know, you know, you understand me. Anyway, I'm gettin' back on the fish business, see. We're out there fishin' like mad for carp. *Carp?* Yeah. *In America?* Then we go back and we cut . . . *Did you catch any?* No, no, no. *How d'you know it was carp you were fishin' then?* Well, I'm tryin' to tell you. Now, we'd go back, we'd go back and we'd eat some chitlins. It was great, it was great, it was great. *You're changing the subject, daddy.* No, no, no. I don't change any subject. Really and truly. The carp wouldn't bite unless we'd eaten chitlins. So we had . . . *What are you using for bait? Your father?* No, baby! *Uncle Henry!* . . . *The balls.* No, no, Babe Ruth! *Oh, his father's balls.* No! baby, don't! I know my old man was great but, I mean, he wasn't all that great. *Hey, Stuff, you still playin' the fiddle through all this?* No. Yeah. Yeah. No. Yeah! Yeah! Yeah! My old man's playin' the flute and Uncle Henry's playin' the guitar. Here I am, standin' up there, tryin' to find out what kind of carp we're goin' to catch. . . . And we haven't caught nothin', you understand me! *But a cold.* No, no, no, didn't even get that. Didn't even get . . . *How are you gonna catch a carp?* Well, I'll tell you. It was like this. You understand? When . . . *Let me pick up on that one, man.* Yeah, yeah. That's all. But I wasn't hip like that, then. But anyway . . . *You were, from your mother's milk. I mean* . . . No, that's the cow's milk! *I'm so*

50

sorry. Well, well, I told you. Didn't I tell you about, didn't I tell you about, my grandfather, owning a great big lot of land? Did I tell you about that? *Yes, you did.* My grandfather owned a whole great big lot of land. And he growed some green grass. Beautiful green grass. *And the cows ate it.* Yeah, but not the kind of grass you think. *Oh, but I know.* Hazelnuts. *Oh, hazelnuts.* Yeah. Yeah. Yeah, yeah. He had some of the finest tea that you ever seen in your life. No really, really. I mean, I'm not kiddin". . . . No, no, tenderleaf tea. Tenderleaf tea, he had. And the cows used to go out there and eat this grass, you know, and one time the milk that they give you . . . I'm asking you, what kind of milk did they give you? . . . *I've had some Jamaican perfume.* That was some of the greatest milk that I have ever tasted in my life. Because . . . *Did it make you high?* No, it didn't make you high. It made you stupid . . . *Now I know.* What? *That explains everything.* Because . . . *A lot of vitamins.* . . . No, there wasn't any vitamins in that milk. *Couscous?* No, no, that wasn't even in the dictionary then. This was in 1834. *How old were you then, Stuff?* . . . *Seven.* Six. You missed it by a year. You understand me? . . . Well, I mean, I mean . . . that's all. That's the way it goes. . . . Shh . . . So . . . *Hey, we're recording Stuff Smith.* So, little old Rosenkrantz and me, we used to drive up to the same river. . . . Yeah, I was there, I was there, I was there . . . We used to drive up to the same river, you know, you know, the Seine. *The Seine?* The Seine is over. . . . *The same one.* The same thing, same thing. *The same sage.* The same thing. That's what I'm tryin' to say. . . . He was busboy on the boat. *Oh God, we're on a boat now.* Yeah! . . . And Oxford. Oxford won that title that year. *But that's England.* No! Cambridge. Sorry. . . . *My God, play this back immediately* . . . *But really, that was a delightful story* . . . *It was so delightful* . . . *We'll play this back.*

End

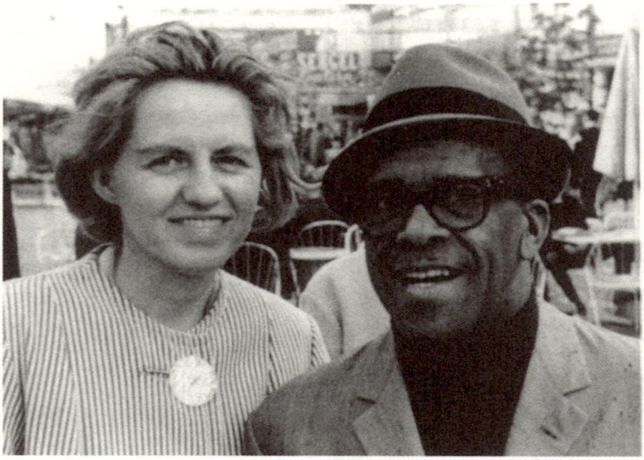

I HOPE GABRIEL LIKES MY MUSIC

GOD, MUSIC & MR WHISKEY

As told by
STUFF SMITH
& written by
LYNN GORDON
nom-de-plume of
Arlene Smith

*Typescript by Mary Lee Hester of first pages
of a lost longer manuscript by Arlene Smith
Los Angeles, 1957 or later*

*Stuff Smith, violinist,
known as the "Peck's Bad Boy of Music",
meets Gabriel, trumpeter, and a man's life changes.
A deep look into the soul of a great musician.
— LG aka AS*

Footnotes by AB

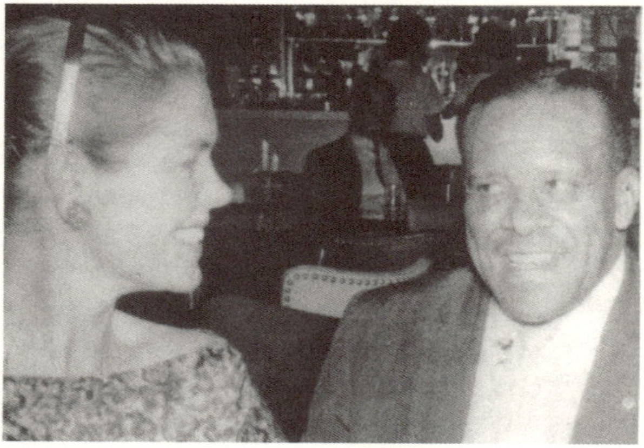

WHEN I woke up and saw my wife and all them doctors standing around me again I shut my eyes fast. I thought, Man, they're going to drag me again, with all that talk. I'd been through all that riff before, too many times. So it took a minute to think back to how I was brought in *this* time.

I'd been drinking nothing but vodka since the last time, 'cause last time it wasn't nothing but whiskey that did it. It couldn't have been the vodka that made me sick this time. I remembered eating some left-over beef this morning (or was it weeks ago—I didn't know how long I'd been in here). I guess it was that beef that I was spitting up, 'cause it was dark brown and didn't look like no blood like my wife kept telling me. I sure was sick and all day got sicker and sicker. I must've passed out because I didn't have any recollection of being brought to the hospital again. I'd *told* my wife not to bring me to no hospital!

I was mad, but I didn't say nothing. I just kept my eyes closed and thought, As soon as they get out of here I'm going to get up and get my clothes on and leave. I'm never going to come to a hospital again. If I'm going to die, like they been telling me every single time I get in here, then I'll die. But I know God won't let me die till it's my time. I figured I'd stop drinking vodka for a while, just till I got on my feet, and then drink the rest of my life, if it was two weeks or twenty years.

But I couldn't keep my eyes shut all day. So I opened them and they jumped on me like I figured they would. What they told me was a shock. They wanted to operate on me. Jack, I started getting *out* of that man's bed! *Nobody* was going to cut open my body, not *my* body! No! Hell No! I wanted no part of that mess and told them so. I was ready to get up out of that bed and fight everybody and show them I wasn't all that sick. Well, man, you know I got out of that hospital as soon as I could, with nobody's permission. I went home and drank lots of milk and chewed up ice cubes like they told me. I was too weak to be up much, even after all the blood transfusions they'd given me, so I sat home and thought. I thought about what a great life I'd had and how I've had a lot of fun, and lots of the fun came from drinking. I could tell you crazy stories all night about things I did and saw when my friends and I were drunk.

Like the time I was so high I fell off the stage at the State and Lake Theatre in Chicago right into the bass drum. And the time we looked around the party and wondered where Art Tatum went and found out he had driven himself home through the streets of New York and we never did figure how a blind man who knew nothing about driving a car could do such a thing. Come to think of it, I was in the car too! Guess his whiskey was driving.

And the time at the Famous Door in Los Angeles when we were so high and got mad at the boss for not paying us on time, and I told the boys, Come on, and we all loaded into a plane and went to New York and we didn't show the next night on the bandstand because we were three thousand miles away and the Union fined us each $500. And the months my friend and I had thirteen empty pints of whiskey stacked in the kitchen every morning and nobody drunk it but us.

And the time Art Tatum and I stayed up for six months playing and drinking all night on the job till four o'clock and drinking and playing all day long until it was time to go back to work and we never hit the bed. And the time my girlfriend drove me home in my brand new Cord because I was too drunk to drive and she hit almost every car on the block on both sides of the street and I woke up to find my Cord completely smashed and didn't care too much 'cause I'd had it a week.

And the time a couple of us had a still on the second floor of an old building and the law raided the place and I dove head first through the second storey window, hit the ground, and got up and left town. And the time in Chicago I was so high my sister couldn't get me to stop shooting my initials in the wall with my .22 and she called The Man and by the time the cops broke in I was sitting at the piano playing "Mother Machree" and gave them a big smile and jived them so pretty they wouldn't believe I would shoot up the place.[1]

And the time I was so drunk I crawled home five blocks on my hands and knees because I couldn't walk. And the time I forgot where I parked my car on the street at the Rose Bowl Game in California and after the game it took us five full hours to find it. And the time in 1951 I was waiting at La Guardia for a plane and they came and asked us how many would volunteer to go on a new jet plane they were experimenting with and me and my juiced self went on and killed a pint of whiskey just as we pulled into Chicago and they hadn't perfected jets yet, I guess, for everybody got off the plane with nosebleeds and ear bleeds and upset stomachs and some had to be carried off and I got off feeling fine and pushed right past the reporters trying to ask me how it was because I never noticed the ride.

I thought about all these things and how they wouldn't have happened except for Mr Whiskey. And there ain't no question— I had a ball. My life had been great and no regrets. I'd been in all the places that counted and for years I had more money than I knew how to spend. I'd had almost every great musician and singer from Bob Crum to Frank Sinatra with me at some time or another and you have to be a musician to know that company like that is greater than kicks in this man's world.

One of my crazy novelty songs and two of my pretty ones had hit No. 1 on the Hit Parade.[2] I had good, close friends in every city and town I'd ever played in and many others besides in every kind of business and every amount of success and I

---

[1] Pianist Helen Smith, eldest of Smith's three older sisters. [2] Smith's "I'se a Muggin'" recorded by him & others; "It's Wonderful", composed with Mitchell Parish, recorded by others; & prob. his recording of "Robins & Roses" by Leslie, Burke.

thank God for them all. Almost every day I meet an old friend I haven't seen in a long while and it's like every day was Christmas. And a wonderful family and good wives and a son twice as tall as me who is really straight and I'm proud to be Dad to. And then the greatest thing of all—Music. And, Man, here I can't tell you anything at all because music starts when words leave off and who tries to talk words about it, is missing the whole point.

Like I said, I thought about all these things and they looked good to me. So there would be no operation and I was ready to die with my drinking boots on because I've never been afraid of anything or anybody and that includes dying. I have tried to be a good Christian all my life because that's the way I was brought up. So God can take me whenever He thinks it's best and I'll be ready.

But the Doc, Dr Pete Reynolds, was a good doctor and a friend and liked to talk about music. So when he asked me to come in for X-rays and some tests so they could study some more about cirrhosis, I went in to see him. I asked him about the operation. He explained the whole situation.

Stuff, he said, if you have this operation you may live a normal lifetime, while without it, you won't have two years.[1] But it's a waste of time for us to operate and a waste of valuable blood donations if you aren't going to stop drinking. He told me about the odds against living through a bleeding like I had went way up every time it happened, so that about the third time around it was something like ten thousand to one. Then he asked me how many times I had hemorrhaged. Well, it had been seven times but I said three. I was afraid Doc would run out of numbers.

All this made me laugh. What did the doctors know anyway? Of course, it was wonderful all the things they can do nowadays,

---

[1] In fact, Smith enjoyed some ten more years, despite relapses.

but it didn't seem to have anything to do with me. Because even if they were right, I wasn't afraid of dying, like I said, and figured that was that. That's what I thought then. I went home and tried to forget about it. I wasn't strong enough to do too much but sit around the house watching TV and listening to records. I had plenty of time to think.

I wasn't paying any attention to what I was stacking on the player, when one of my old records struck home. It was the one called "I Hope Gabriel Likes My Music". I began thinking— Would he? I know it sounds crazy, but I couldn't get it off my mind. I think God was trying to tell me something by keeping the idea buzzing in my head. You see, my music has been my life—my real life and if my music wasn't accepted at the Pearly Gates, then something was wrong and I *wasn't* ready. This was a new idea to me, because I'd given my whole life to writing and playing the best music I could. I began thinking back over my whole musical life.

I began thinking way back to a house by the river in Masillon, Ohio. My Dad had a barbershop on the ground floor and we lived above it. It was a nice house with a lot of good memories for me. Our family was a very close, very loving family. But my mother made my three sisters and myself behave very strictly so that we were brought up right.

The barbershop was fun to be in, even after I got old enough to do the shoeshines, because it was a man's world and a change from the company of three sisters. But after the shop closed and Dad and me and Mr Henry—our friend—went down to the river was the best time.[1] 'Cause then we would sit out of sight in a little place . . .

[1] The Uncle Henry of "Stuff Smith Slept Here", cf. p.49

End

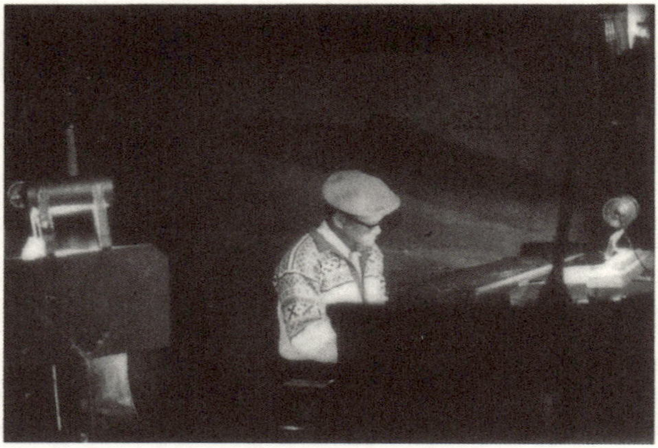

THE HUMAN SIDE OF JAZZ

AN AUTOBIOGRAPHICAL BEGINNING

Narrated by
STUFF SMITH

*Recorded by Eva Løgager
for a proposed autobiography at
Camp du T.C.F., outskirts of Paris
on three occasions June 1967*

Asterix denotes laughter

Transcribed & Newly Edited by AB

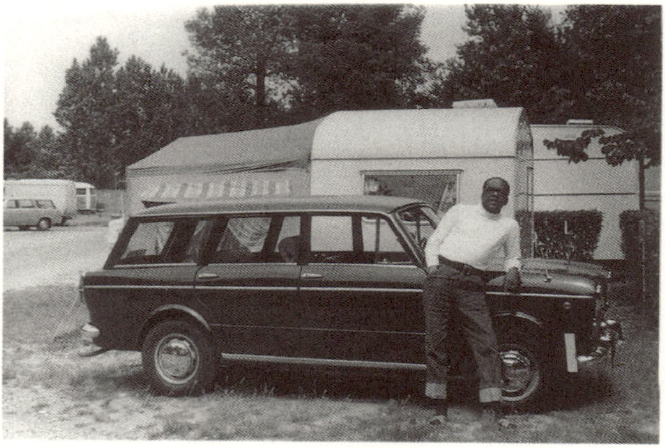

ALL you fine people. I *hope* that you take time out to read this book that I'm going to try to put down . . .

I love beauty. I don't love sorrow. I love beauty. Beauty. And, when I say beauty, that takes in all the category of music. The sweetness of music. The harshness. The roughness. The anything that you can think of, is right there, in that one word called beauty.

I love beautiful women. Like my wife. You know. She's beautiful. But she's devilish . . .[1] We're going to show you something that you, I mean we're going to show you something in music that you probably didn't know . . .

Number one. I am a violinist. I'm not a fiddle player. * I'm a violinist. I play the violin my way. That's the way I think it should be played. I mean according to the type of music that I play. Now, when I was a young boy my father, who was a musician, my sisters, they were, they were doing pretty good. And I was doing pretty good. So, so, I had my first escapade of hearing some good music, which I love . . .

I love jazz. And they're trying to tear up jazz, trying to make a symphony of jazz. But they can't do it. If you can't pat your foot you ain't got jazz. That's what I'm saying. Now, they've done everything to jazz. They stood still with jazz these days. these boys that are playing. They learn the chorus of a record that some other fella has made and then they come out, and they play that, on their instrument. But don't let them play anything else because they don't *know* nothing else. That's the reason I say good jazz is the jazz that's come from the bottom of the pit. When I say the bottom of the pit that means guys like Joe Venuti. Eddie Lang. Red Allen. Bix Beiderbecke. Coleman Hawkins. Fletcher Henderson. And the old boss, Louis Armstrong. That's good jazz. Frankie Trumbauer. I can name a gang of them. All

---

[1] Eva Løgager, Smith's companion during the last year and a half of his life.

the boys that play good jazz. And good jazz you cannot beat. If you want to pat your foot. If you don't want to pat your foot go to some symphony * and listen to Beethoven. He's good too. He *was* good, I mean. But anyway, our subject is only jazz. Swing we call it. After Benny Goodman. That learned a few licks from our boy in Chicago.[1] * He called it swing. What did I tell you! There's nothing like jazz. It's going to stay here. They're trying to get rid of it. But it's going to stay here. Because it's in your heart. It's in your feet. it's in your blood. And that's the thing that counts. Other things are great. Other things are really great. Like your symphonies give you, give you a menu. To let you know what's happening. And this and that and the other. But in jazz you just come and sit down and listen. And if it satisfies you, and you pat your feet, that is jazz . . .

Now, you take the case of a young man that I know. A very fine looking little fat trumpet player. * He's the swingin'est thing on earth. His name is Roy Eldridge. We met years and years ago when I was playing with Alphonso Trent's band. Somewhere in Ohio. he was playing with Speed Webb. And he had *all* of his keys, the top of his keys, taken off. He took them off. And he chopped them down. He chopped down his mouthpiece. To make it real thin. So you get higher notes. And boy, we used to stand back and look at this cat play. Now that boy could play. And now he's turned out to be one of the best in the world. Boy, that's my boy. That's the swingin'est cat in the world. He can swing . . . It don't mean a thing if you ain't got Roy Eldridge. * That's my boy. That's my buddy.

Now, for instance, you take old [Russell] Procope. Procope who played with John Kirby before. And he played very beautiful. He's a swinging little cat, too. All them cats. Cats I'm talking

[1] Jimmie Noone.

about can swing, man. I ain't bullshitting. I'm talking about the real swing.

Take Jonah Jones. That old [expletive]. * He can swing his ass off. * He's got a swinging little band. We were together for about seventeen years. from Buffalo. He used to be with Jimmie Lunceford. Then he came over to me. In Buffalo. We had a good little band too. We had us a good little band. You bet your life. Casa Loma boys used to come in and hear it and say, What you doing here in Buffalo? Why don't you go to New York? Why the hell should I go to New York when I live in Buffalo and I'm doing pretty fair? You understand me?

Now, there's another little old boy that can swing his ass off. His name is Peanuts Holland. He's right here in Europe. He's in Stockholm. Sweden. He played in my band. He could blow like a dog. Yeah, yeah. All of them boys. Vic Dickenson. They all played with me. And I played with them. I mean musically. * We'll put it that way. I think that's the way to put it. Musically.

Willie Smith. Young man who's just passed away. About a month ago. he was one of my best friends. He was supposed to marry my sister-in-law. But he never got around to it. He went to California. Left Jimmie Lunceford and went to California and joined up with Harry James. Harry James is one of the [?]readin'est trumpet players I ever saw in my life. * And can play! But Willie Smith is one of the greatest first also players you ever heard in your life. Outside of Johnny Hodges. There's a boy. There's a boy that plays melody and he plays swing like a dog. And his notes are truly pure. As I said before, I love beauty, and he's got it. And there's another boy who plays beautiful trombone named Dicky Wells. He was with Basie . . .

So there you are. Them's your boys. We used to have a good time back in those days. In those days when old . . . Fats Waller * would be in front of the Music House there on Broadway. And he would say, I'd turn the corner, getting off the subway, and I'd turn the corner, and there would be Fats. And he says, Stuff! Draw! So we drew. he would have him a half pint of gin and I'd have me a half pint of gin too. And we drew at each other. * And he says, Let's go somewhere and play . . . So we did. We used to do all that. We had a good time. There's a playing young boy. And a good composer. You know. Those were the days when a musician enjoyed playing. He didn't play for money. He played for himself and for his friends. He was *supposed* to play because it was in his blood. It was in his mind. And in his heart. And in his soul. And in his sleep. And that's what we had. We had the beat in our feet. That's for sure.

And, when Duke wrote this song "It Don't Mean a Thing If It Ain't Got that Swing", a certain man, a piano player, we call him Will'e Slip the Lion,[1] he says, Now Stuff, that is *right*. It don't mean a thing if you ain't got that swing. So, we used to go and jam up there in New York, by the Lafayette Theatre. And play until next morning.

Now, there's one man who was really astonishing. He and Fatha Hines. Fatha Hines was in Chicago. And this young fella, who was about eighteen years old then, came to Chicago and played *beautiful* piano. The greatest piano I ever heard in my life. He came to Chicago. And Earl Hines says, They tell me you can play piano. So he says, Yeah, I can play a little bit. * So he went on. They went downstairs. A place in Chicago . . . The Grand Terrace . . . So they went down there. And Earl Hines got on the piano and started playing "Body and Soul". And he started playing. So, he played it in D flat, which is five flats, which is the original key. He played in there. And when he finished, he says, Now, will you play this? he says, Yes. But I ain't going to stay in D flat. He says, I'm going to start from C and take it all the way

[1] Willie the Lion Smith.

through. C. B flat. B natural. A natural. E natural. G natural. F sharp. *All* them keys I'm going to play in. And Earl Hines says, Aw, no. He says, Aw, yeah. So he sat down. His name was Art Tatum. The greatest pianist that ever lived. Art Tatum. As far as I'm concerned. Yes. Now, that is jazz. That is jazz that you can't forget. That's jazz that stays with you. And will *be* with you as long as you got two feet to stand on. And if you haven't got two feet to stand on you got *one* foot to stand on. But you can still pat that one foot. Believe me. And this boy named Art Tatum could play it. He is one of the greatest musicians that ever lived. And one of the greatest I ever played with. And I practically played with them all. But he is the boss. He and Duke.

Duke Ellington. One evening, when I got through playing at my club, I was with Charlie Barnet. He's a fine tenor saxophone player. And Charlie says, Let's go in, Stuff, and have us a little beer before we go home. I says, Sure. And he says, Incidentally, old Duke Ellington's playing over here. This was Los Angeles, you know. I says, Sure enough. * So, we went over there. And when we got there Duke was blowing like a dog. Ray Nance was playing the violin. Johnny Hodges was playing the horn. And, my boy [Harry Carney] the baritone. He was playing his baritone. And everything was fine, you know. So I says, Duke, May I play a number with you? He says, Sure, Stuff. Come on here. Sit down here and play something. So I went and got my beat-up amplifier * and set up on the stand. Plugged it in, to the socket. And Duke says, C sharp. Now what the hell I know he's talking about C sharp! Well, he says, You Got it? C sharp. OK. All right. And we start playing "C-Jam Blues". And we played. We played it for about a half hour. Joe Louis is sitting out in the audience! And he always wanted to be a violin player. Joe Louis. Bless his soul. I love that guy.[1] And so we sat out there and

---

[1] At least one photo is extant of Joe Louis sporting a violin.

67

played "C-Jam Blues". And I had never played "C-Jam Blues" like that in my life. Every time I turned round there was another sharp. * So I got the sharps played.

Oh yeah, that's jazz. Pure jazz. Not this jazz that these cats figure out there way. I mean they stand up there and don't move their body and they don't feel. I don't know how they feel. But to me it looks like it is very *discouraging*. To stand up there and play for the audience. And the audience don't know what the hell you're playing. And they stand up there with their feet flat. They've got their horn in their mouth and they know about three songs. You get them off of them three songs they don't know *nothing*. That ain't jazz! Believe me. You'll find that out, later. What I'm telling you . . . is correct. Ask Timme Rosenkrantz. He knows. He knows jazz. That's one sure thing about old Tim. And we love him for that. He knows jazz. There's a few other boys who know jazz. And when you've got jazz, you've got it . . .

There's another little fellow, and he's gone away too. He's one of the finest in the jazz in the country and he was my friend, very good friend. His name was Hot Lips Page. He came from Kansas City. A fine trumpet player and a good singer. And a good entertainer all the way around.

You know what I should do is tell you about these boys that I have been speaking about. Well, we start with, let me see. Henry Red Allen. Henry Red Allen was on the boats in St Louis. Strekfus Steamboat Line, with his father. And both of them were playing trumpet, hm. He was on the *J. S.* [ss *J. S. DeLux*]. That's the name of the boat. And Alphonso Trent's band, who I was a member of, we were on the steamer *St Paul*. Now, Henry Red Allen's boat used to go to New Orleans. Well, we never went to New Orleans. We'd always go north. And give our little excursion. And every Monday night Louis Armstrong would come from Chicago, and play on the steamer *St Paul*. And we would have us a ball, hm. That cat would come down the street and you thought, ah, President Roosevelt was walking down the street. Everybody enjoyed Louis so much and loved him so much. I just can remember. He had on a camel's hair coat and a camel's hair cap. And he walked up to the steamer, says, Boys, and he said, is this it? And we said, Yeah, Louis, come on in Pops. And we had a ball that night.[1] *

Now, let me tell you something about Charlie Shavers. I'm taking all the trumpet players now. Charlie Shavers. He's real fast on his horn. And plays fine. He don't miss nothing. And he's a good arranger. As a matter of fact, he kept John Kirby's band going, he and Billy Kyle, for about three years. There's some good arrangers.

Now, let's talk about saxophone players. There's an old beat up fat cat named Ben Webster. He's in Amsterdam now. He's a fine boy. He's like a little baby when he hasn't been drinking. But when he's drinking look out, run, run, you hear me, you run! He's the roughest cat you ever saw in your life, hm. But he's still my pal.

Another tenor saxophone player named Don Stovall. No! I don't mean Don Stovall. I mean Don Byas. Don Stovall is an alto player. He's a good boy. But Don Byas, he and Ben Webster, are in the same class. Only Don's a little smaller. Don is one of these deep sea divers, who likes to go under the water, with his rubber suit on, and catch fish with a spear. * I told him, Go on down there, Jack, I ain't coming with you. You understand me?

Now, there's another tenor player. His name is Joe Thomas. He used to to be with Jimmie Lunceford. And he went to Kansas City and got married. And the girl that he married, her father

[1] cf. note p.12

died and left him a great big block of a funeral parlor. Now, who wants a funeral parlor? But he was there! * Joe Thomas. There's my boy too. And he can blow.

There's another one. Hal Singer. We can't forget him. He can blow too. Ah yeah. He's here in Paris. He's not playing with me. But he's playing right around the corner. At a place called ... the Chat qui pêche. I'm saying all these French words. I don't know what the hell they are. But he's a good boy. We're going to play together, the twenty-fourth of this month, in the southern part of France. That's him.

Now, let me see. There's another tenor player. His name is Ironjaws. From New York. Plays his can off. He was here. At the Montmartre. Did very well in Copenhagen. And he was doing very well. And he did very well. He can blow too.[1]

There's another tenor player. From Little Rock, Arkansas. His name is Hayes Pillars. From the Jeter and Pillars band. Hm, hm. He can blow. All them cats can blow. They're solid musicians. They ain't these over the night musicians like you're hearing. You've been brainwashed. That's the trouble with you. All of you have been brainwashed. You little youngsters. You should go back and hear the boys and learn the real jazz. It's true, what I'm saying. And that's the thing that counts. If you want to pat your foot, that's it. This other mess they're laying down, man, I'm sorry.

Now, the swingin'est band, little band, I ever heard in my life, was called the Savoy Sultans. They played at the Savoy Ballroom in New York City. And boy, all them cats could blow like a dog. Yeah ... And there was another little group called the Five Spirits of Rhythm. Now, Leo Watson was the greatest scat singer you ever heard in your life. That's true. And we used to play together. Yeah, that boy was something.

[1] Smith may mean Eddie Lockjaw Davies who played in Europe spring 1967.

Now, we'll take Miss Ella Fitzgerald. I gave her her first commercial. On radio. In New York City. Called *Let's Listen to Luciden.* That was eye drops, you know. And Ella Fitzgerald was the vocalist. And our arranger was the fella that wrote "Stomping at the Savoy." His name was, hm, I'll think of it and tell you about it later. Anyway, we had half of Chick's band. Chick Webb. We had his brass section. We had Cab Calloway's reed section. Then I had my band stuck in there. Edgar Sampson is that boy's name. That was the arranger of the band. And we had some pretty good arrangements. And we used to hit on that program quite a length of time. So, finally, we made our little loot, and got off of it, and went back to the Onyx Club, to start playing again.[1]

So there you are. One of these days I'm going to tell you about myself. One of these days. How I started in this field of music . . . I just want you to know the boys. And the boys that can really swing. The real boys. Pure at Heart, we call them. Pure at Heart. So we'll see you later . . .

[1] cf. note p.35

End

Violin Studies by Anthony Barnett
available from the same UK publisher & US distributor

Desert Sands
The Recordings and Performances of Stuff Smith
An Annotated Discography & Biographical Source Book
with supplement
Up Jumped the Devil
1995/1998

Black Gypsy
The Recordings of Eddie South
An Annotated Discography & Itinerary
1999

Substantial corrections and additions to
Desert Sands/Up Jumped the Devil & Black Gypsy
are included in later volumes of
Fable Bulletin: Violin Improvisation Studies
available only from the UK publisher
four volumes in thirteen parts
1993–2000
with updates from 2001 onwards online at
www.abar.net

Details of previously unreleased violin recordings
by Stuff Smith, Ray Perry, Eddie South a.o.
on CD AB Fable & on
Mosaic, Soundies, Frog, Storyville
will also be found on our website